D1372354

EDGE BOOKS™

The Real World of Pirates

THE HISTORY OF PIRATES

FROM PRIVATEERS TO OUTLAWS

By Allison Lassieur

Consultant:
Sarah Knott, Director
Pirate Soul Museum
Key West, Florida

Capstone
press®

Mankato, Minnesota

Edge Books are published by Capstone Press,
151 Good Counsel Drive, P.O. Box 669, Mankato, Minnesota 56002.
www.capstonepress.com

Library of Congress Cataloging-in-Publication Data
Lassieur, Allison.
    The history of pirates: from privateers to outlaws / by Allison Lassieur.
    p. cm.—(Edge Books. The real world of pirates)
    Summary: "Describes the history of pirates, including the reasons people became
pirates and why the Golden Age of Piracy ended"—Provided by publisher.
    Includes bibliographical references and index.
    ISBN-13: 978-0-7368-6423-7 (hardcover)
    ISBN-10: 0-7368-6423-7 (hardcover)
    1. Pirates—History—Juvenile literature. I. Title. II. Series.
G535.L29 2007
910.4'5—dc22   2006006995

Editorial Credits
Angie Kaelberer, editor; Thomas Emery, designer; Jason Knudson, illustrator;
    Kim Brown, colorist; Wanda Winch and Charlene Deyle, photo researchers

Photo Credits
Corbis/Bettmann, 15
Delaware Art Museum/Howard Pyle Manuscript Collection, Helen Farr Sloan Library,
    The Pirates Christmas - A Scene in the Town Jail, published in Harper's Weekly,
    December 1893 (Detail), 5
Mary Evans Picture Library, 8
(c) National Maritime Museum, London/Hendrick Cornelisz Vroom, 25
North Wind Picture Archives, 13
Peter Newark's Historical Pictures, 7, 21, 23; Military Pictures, 10; Pictures, 17, 27,
    26–27
Rick Reeves, 18
ZUMA Press/TCS/Eric Pasquier, 29

1 2 3 4 5 6 11 10 09 08 07 06

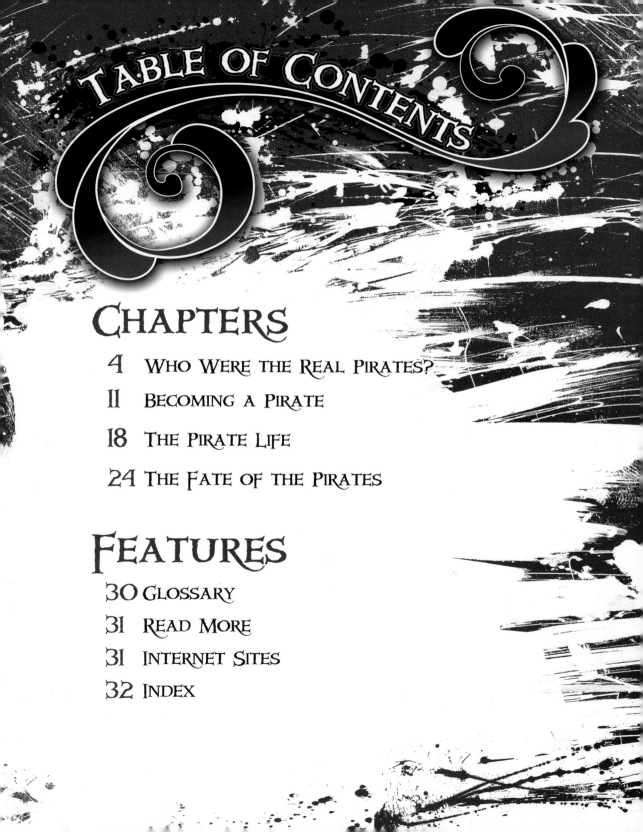

TABLE OF CONTENTS

CHAPTERS

FEATURES

Chapter One

WHO WERE THE REAL PIRATES?

On July 12, 1726, citizens of Boston gathered on the island of Nick's Mate in the Charles River. Pirate William Fly was to be hanged for his terrible crimes at sea. Fly and his crew had mutinied against their captain by taking over their ship. Fly killed the captain. He and his crew then attacked several other ships and stole their cargo.

Learn About:
- Death of a pirate
- Golden Age of Piracy
- Jolly Roger flag

Pirates who were caught faced long jail sentences or worse.

5

When Fly appeared, the people were shocked. He didn't seem upset or afraid. Instead, he smiled and carried flowers. He climbed the stairs to the gallows and took charge. Fly saw that the hangman's rope wasn't knotted correctly. He offered to teach the hangman how to do it better!

Finally, everything was ready. Fly turned to the crowd and began to speak. But did he apologize for his crimes? Did he ask forgiveness? No! Instead, he spoke about the harsh treatment that men at sea faced. He wished captains would treat their sailors better. He hoped sailors would be paid fairly for their work. He said that harsh treatment forced many sailors to become pirates.

Fly had barely finished speaking when the gallows floor dropped. Fly was dead at age 27. He had been a pirate for only two months.

Hanging was a common punishment for crimes of piracy.

Many pirate ships flew the Jolly Roger flag, which was decorated with a skull and crossbones.

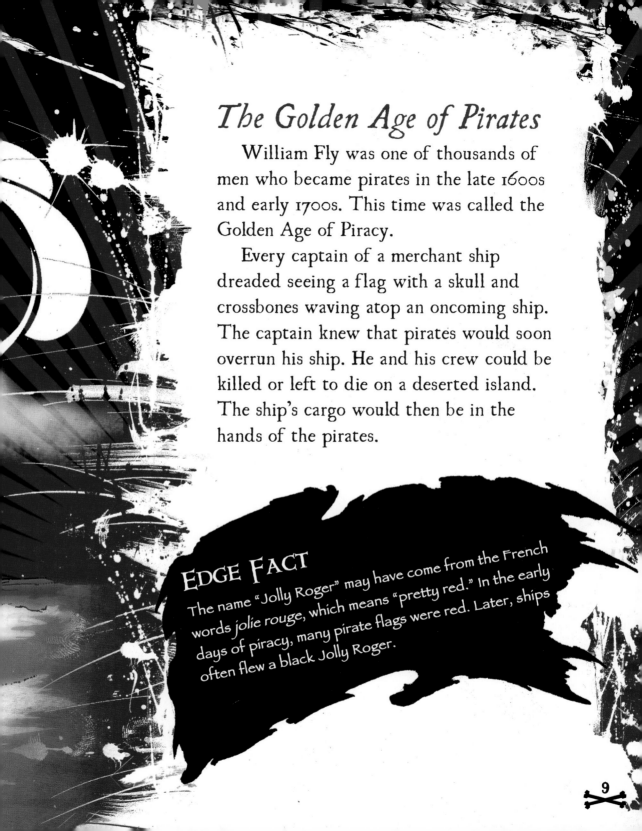

The Golden Age of Pirates

William Fly was one of thousands of men who became pirates in the late 1600s and early 1700s. This time was called the Golden Age of Piracy.

Every captain of a merchant ship dreaded seeing a flag with a skull and crossbones waving atop an oncoming ship. The captain knew that pirates would soon overrun his ship. He and his crew could be killed or left to die on a deserted island. The ship's cargo would then be in the hands of the pirates.

EDGE FACT

The name "Jolly Roger" may have come from the French words *jolie rouge*, which means "pretty red." In the early days of piracy, many pirate flags were red. Later, ships often flew a black Jolly Roger.

In the 1600s and 1700s,
European navies battled for
control of the New World.

Chapter Two

BECOMING A PIRATE

The late 1600s and early 1700s were a time of change. European explorers had discovered vast amounts of gold, timber, and wildlife in North and South America. These areas were called the New World.

People in England, Spain, France, and other European countries wanted the New World's rich resources. Ships loaded with treasures sailed back and forth across the Atlantic Ocean. European countries went to war over control of the Americas. They used their navies to attack one another's ships at sea.

Learn About:
- The New World
- Life in the navy
- Ways to piracy

Ships and their supplies were expensive. Governments sometimes hired private shipowners. Government leaders gave the owners letters of marque. These documents gave shipowners permission to attack enemy ships. In return, the owners shared the captured treasure with the government. Men who attacked other ships in the service of their country were called privateers, or legal pirates.

Privateers experienced the excitement of wealth and adventure. After the wars ended, many continued stealing on their own. They became outlaw pirates.

From Sailor to Pirate

Other people took different paths to becoming pirates. Even though many governments had great wealth, thousands of men and women in Europe couldn't earn enough money to survive. One of the worst jobs was a navy sailor.

Most European countries had large navies, even though few men volunteered for the job. Groups called navy press gangs kidnapped men and forced them to become sailors. This practice, called conscription, was common throughout Europe. Most conscripted sailors hated what had happened to them.

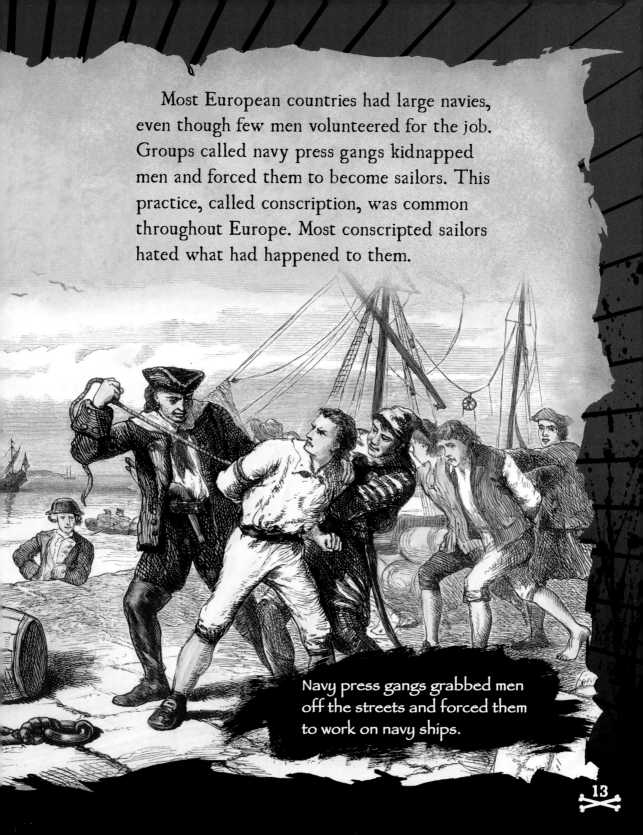

Navy press gangs grabbed men off the streets and forced them to work on navy ships.

Life at Sea

The conditions on navy ships were terrible. Many captains beat and tortured their sailors. The food was bad and the work hours were long.

For many sailors, the cruel treatment was more than they could stand. Some sailors killed their captains and took over their ships as pirates. Others looked for pirate ships they could join.

Life on a pirate ship was usually better than life on a navy ship. Pirate captains usually treated their sailors fairly. But the best part of a pirate's life was the hope of valuable treasure. With every raid or attack, pirates had the chance to become rich beyond their dreams.

Pirates had more freedom than navy sailors, but they still had to follow their captains' orders.

15

Forming a Pirate Crew

Most pirate crews formed in one of two ways. One was by mutiny. After a mutiny, the sailors could stay with the pirates or follow the captain. Most chose to stay. Those who chose to leave were often killed or were set adrift on the ocean with their captain, never to be seen again. If the pirates were in good moods, they sometimes gave crew members small boats so they could return to their homes.

Other people joined existing pirate crews. When pirates captured a ship, they usually invited the crew to join them. Most men chose to join the pirates.

Sometimes, the pirates even gave the ship back to its crew members. These sailors could become pirates on their own, or they could sail home.

Edge Fact

After a mutiny, the crew sometimes marooned the captain on a deserted island. He was left on the island with no food or water.

Pirates launched rowboats to reach and capture merchant ships.

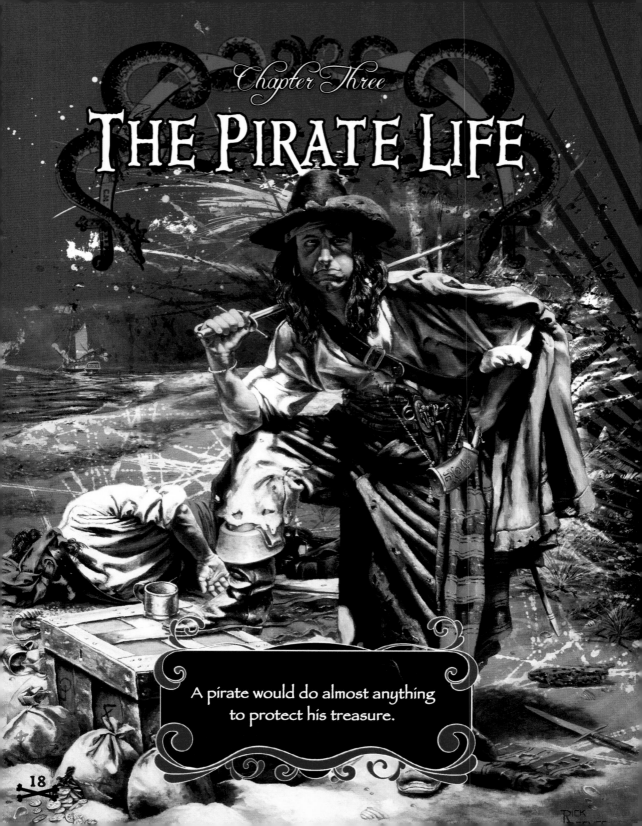

Chapter Three
THE PIRATE LIFE

A pirate would do almost anything
to protect his treasure.

The life of a pirate wasn't fun or glamorous. Most pirates were ordinary men who were tired of being poor and mistreated. They longed for respect and fairness.

The Pirate Code

Pirates wanted to be sure life was fair for everyone on their ships. Every pirate ship drew up a set of rules, called articles. Each pirate was honor-bound to follow the Pirate Code.

The Pirate Code said each crew member had an equal say in decisions. Each man was part of the pirate council. The council voted on who would become captain. The articles set rules about sharing food and work. They also listed punishments for breaking the rules.

Learn About:
- Pirate rules
- Crew jobs
- Notorious pirates

After pirates attacked a ship, the Pirate Code gave strict instructions for how the loot would be divided. Each pirate got at least one share. Some pirates got more, based on their skills and duties.

For most pirates, it was the first time they had ever been treated fairly. They were well paid for their hard work. Best of all, no one ordered them around.

A pirate's life often was short and full of violence. But for many, it was much better than what they had before.

The Power of the Crew

A pirate captain led the pirates during fighting or when the ship was being chased. But he had no other special rights. The captain slept with the crew and ate the same food. If the captain did something that the rest of the pirates didn't like, they could vote him out and choose a new captain.

Each pirate received at least one
share of the captured treasure.

The most respected man on a pirate ship was the quartermaster. Like the captain, the quartermaster was an elected position. He was usually the best-liked and most trusted pirate.

The quartermaster handed out food and loot to each pirate. He also maintained order. If pirates had a problem with the captain or another sailor, they went to the quartermaster to settle it.

EDGE FACT

Many pirate codes included rules about paying pirates who had been injured. Payment was in pieces of eight, which were Spanish silver coins. Injuries to right legs and arms were worth more money than left limbs because most people are right-handed.

Famous Pirates

Edward "Blackbeard" **Teach** was one of the most feared pirates of all time. His nickname came from the thick black beard that covered his face. He captured at least 40 ships and killed hundreds of people. Blackbeard was killed in a bloody battle off the coast of North Carolina in 1718.

British Navy officer Robert Maynard (right) killed Blackbeard (left).

Sam Bellamy began his career as a sailor with the English Navy. His huge ship the *Whydah* was equipped with 28 guns. In 1717, Bellamy died when the *Whydah* sank near Cape Cod, Massachusetts.

Bartholomew "Black Bart" Roberts is believed to have captured about 400 ships during his three-year career. He died during a battle with a British warship off the coast of Africa in 1722.

Chapter Four

THE FATE OF THE PIRATES

During the Golden Age of Piracy, many cities in the American colonies tolerated pirates. At the time, Great Britain controlled the colonies. The British government permitted the colonists to buy goods only from Britain. Americans were forced to pay high prices for British goods. Pirates brought cheaper goods to sell and riches to spend.

But by the mid-1700s, piracy was less profitable. Ships still carried cargo of gold, silver, and goods across the Atlantic Ocean. But the cargo was less than it had been just a few years before.

By law, American colonists could trade only with British ships. Pirate ships gave colonists another opportunity for trade.

Learn About:
- Piracy profits
- Laws against piracy
- Modern piracy

New Laws

Governments also helped end piracy. Many countries passed harsh laws that punished anyone who bought from or sold to a pirate. Officials who once allowed pirates in their cities now arrested them.

Also, most European countries had settled their differences. They combined forces to get rid of pirates. One by one, pirates and pirate ships were hunted down and captured.

By the mid-1700s, pirates were likely to be captured and punished for their crimes.

Governments even realized that the terrible conditions aboard navy ships encouraged many men to become pirates. Laws were created to protect sailors. Sailors received better pay and working conditions. These reforms kept men from joining pirate crews. By 1750, the Golden Age of Piracy was over.

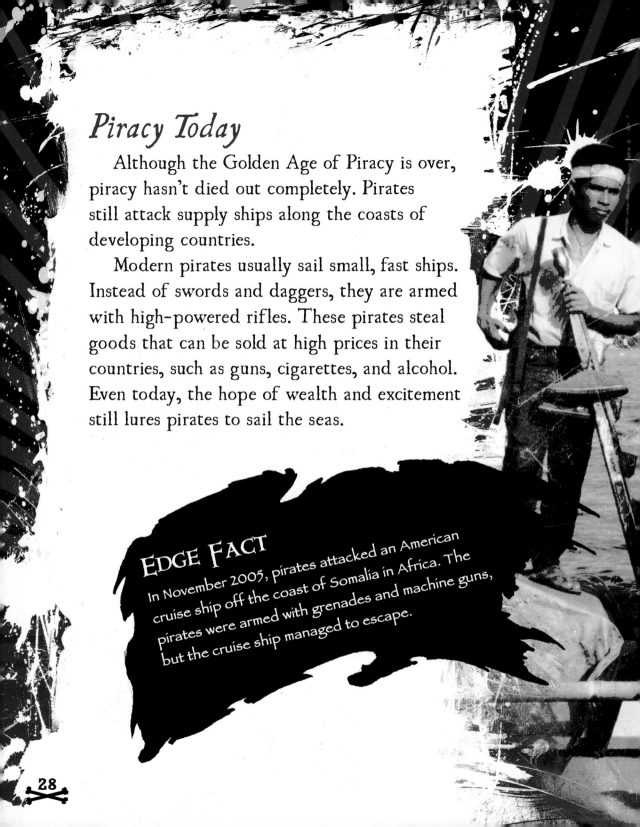

Piracy Today

Although the Golden Age of Piracy is over, piracy hasn't died out completely. Pirates still attack supply ships along the coasts of developing countries.

Modern pirates usually sail small, fast ships. Instead of swords and daggers, they are armed with high-powered rifles. These pirates steal goods that can be sold at high prices in their countries, such as guns, cigarettes, and alcohol. Even today, the hope of wealth and excitement still lures pirates to sail the seas.

EDGE FACT

In November 2005, pirates attacked an American cruise ship off the coast of Somalia in Africa. The pirates were armed with grenades and machine guns, but the cruise ship managed to escape.

Modern-day pirates in the Philippines search the South China Sea for victims.

Glossary

cargo (KAR-goh)—the goods carried by a ship

conscription (kuhn-SKRIP-shun)—a forced military draft

council (KOUN-suhl)—a group of leaders chosen to look after the interests of a larger group

loot (LOOT)—stolen goods or treasure

mutiny (MYOOT-uh-nee)—a revolt against the captain of a ship

navy (NAY-vee)—the military sea force of a country

privateer (prye-vuh-TEER)—a person who owns a ship licensed to attack and steal from other ships

quartermaster (KWOR-tur-mass-tur)—a ship's officer who makes sure the captain's orders are carried out and that supplies are distributed among the crew

Read More

Butterfield, Moira. *Pirates and Smugglers*. Kingfisher Knowledge. Boston: Kingfisher, 2005.

Lewis, J. Patrick. *Blackbeard, the Pirate King*. Washington, D.C.: National Geographic Society, 2006.

Walker, Richard. *The Barefoot Book of Pirates*. New York: Barefoot Books, 2004.

Internet Sites

FactHound offers a safe, fun way to find Internet sites related to this book. All of the sites on FactHound have been researched by our staff.

Here's how:

1. Visit *www.facthound.com*

2. Choose your grade level.

3. Type in this book ID **0736864237** for age-appropriate sites. You may also browse subjects by clicking on letters, or by clicking on pictures and words.

4. Click on the **Fetch It** button.

FactHound will fetch the best sites for you!

Index